GRAFFITI LANE

A Poetry Collection

Kelly Van Nelson

Copyright © 2019 by **Kelly Van Nelson**

All rights reserved. No part of this publication may be reproduced, distributed or transmitted in any form or by any means, without prior written permission.

Kelly Van Nelson/Making Magic Happen Press
Perth/Western Australia
www.mmhpress.com

Publisher's Note: This is a work of fiction. Names, characters, places, and incidents are a product of the author's imagination. Locales and public names are sometimes used for atmospheric purposes. Any resemblance to actual people, living or dead, or to businesses, companies, events, institutions, or locales is completely coincidental.

Graffiti Lane/ Kelly Van Nelson. -- 1st ed.

ISBN 978-0-6484803-4-1 (hc)

ISBN 978-0-6484803-5-8 (sc)

ISBN 978-0-6484803-6-5 (e)

For Shaun, Kayin and Imani.
You are the colour in my life.
xxx

FROM THE AUTHOR

As a published author of novels and short stories, I shied away from poetry for many years. For some reason it scared me. All that academic talk of stanzas, metre and form is enough to break any writer into a cold sweat. Eventually though, something made me start scribbling down insights and phrases – haphazard daytime observations or thoughts that churned in my head and caused bouts of insomnia at night. It expanded into verse, mainly written in the closet, never letting a single word see the light of day. Then, in 2009, I wrote a poem called *Repudiated Miracle* which was published in a UK poetry anthology and a new-found confidence was born.

I started putting together a series of poems about being the underdog. Growing up in a council estate in Newcastle-upon-Tyne, my childhood was as far removed from a silver spoon upbringing as one can get. The kind where every surface was made of concrete and there was no safety net in the park. Not long into my teenage years we moved to a new house, across the Tyne River to the other side of town, which also meant moving high schools. I was the new girl on the block in a public school where I didn't know a soul. Luckily, I made some amazing friends, identical twins who remain my besties today and several others I am still connected with from the other side of the world. On the downside, I was bullied. Never physically, but name calling in the corridor was a daily occurrence. The words thrown my way were not particularly vicious, but the repetitive onslaught wore me down, until one day I snapped in PE and punched a girl who was the main instigator of the torment. I certainly don't condone violent retaliation in this type of situation, there are many other ways to get support, but that was the end of the bullying for me.

What I gained from the experience (apart from a week suspended from school), was an inner strength that has stayed with me right through my adult years. A thick skin, a sense of resilience and a steely willpower that is my ultimate super power. Without a doubt, that harsh period spent coping with being on the receiving end of such negative behaviour helped me become the writer I am today; one consumed by the need to speak out at anything inequitable, always people watching, analysing human behaviour, and jotting down random notes about life as I see it through my unfiltered lens.

The poems started to flow and a theme formed around the concept of big bullies; from being kicked down through ill-treatment, to finding ways to bounce back, rise again, and ultimately going full-throttle to the fly-high position intended by destiny. Inspiration came thick and fast. I started seeing the broader effects of intimidation and discrimination spilling down every alley I peered along. Teenage bullying in schools, corporate bullying and harassment, domestic violence, gender inequity and marginalisation, mental health issues and suicide. I began to play with stanzas (yes, stanzas!), and rhyme, trying out new styles of traditional, shadow, and freeform poetry, and the basis of this collection was formed.

Inspiration for the *Graffiti Lane* title came from many, many trips to Melbourne. I've always been drawn to the grittiness of urban life, something that stems from my roots growing up in the North East of England. The beauty in the graffiti of the Melbourne laneways is incredible, a credit to the powers that be, who zoned off dedicated areas for street artists to use the walls as a blank canvas. The results are a colourful kaleidoscope representing freedom of speech and expression. Everything from simple TAGs stating one's identity for the world to see, to complex and intricate portraits sprayed on brick, and finally to social and political statements tackling current affairs. Each piece fizzes with uncensored talent, making a walk along the Melbourne laneways an assault on the senses (with a treasure hunt for elusive Banksy works of street art thrown in).

We all have something to say, but listening and acting on the unjust is just as important as holding a megaphone. It's easy to turn a blind eye on bullying or to let a cry for help fall on deaf ears. To play a role in helping the underdog to fly high requires far more concerted effort.

As part of my corporate work, I've been fortunate enough to be a key note speaker in several schools and universities on important topics such as self-motivation, dealing with bullying, diversity, and promoting career options in the Science, Technology, Engineering and Mathematics (STEM) industry for high school girls, where female representation is low. If just one student walks away from those sessions enthused and with a new lease of life, then my work as a creative artist is done. The same goes if one reader finds solace in a poem contained in this compilation.

Graffiti Lane is my blank canvas filled with an eclectic mix of raw ramblings, poems, pitfalls and dreams. I hope you like it.

Kelly

xxx

CONTENTS

KICKED DOWN 1
   Pink Bubbles 3
   Nettles 4
   Smell the Roses 5
   When the Bell Tolls 6
   Swipe 7
   Lost Diamond 8
   Obey my Command 9
   Greased Palm 10
   Candy Floss 12
   What Might Have Been 13
   Glass Half Empty 14
   Defaced 15
   Eggshells 16
   Play the Hand 18
   Aqua Vitae 20
   Night Terrors 22
   Dinner for One 23
   Corporal Punishment 24
   Dog Days are Over 25
   Ker Plunk 26
   Repudiated Miracle 27
   Tight Spot 28
   The Tuxedo Princess 29
   New Kid on the Block 30

- Mirror, Mirror 31
- Did He Know? 32
- Snake Charmer 34
- The Jester 35
- # 36
- SPEAK OUT 37
  - Faceless Without Art 39
  - Bully 'Four' You 40
  - Sparkle 41
  - Diversity 42
  - Big Bullies, Small Minds 43
  - Talk Back 44
  - Inside Out 45
  - The Whistleblower 46
  - Against All Odds 48
  - Through the Eyes of the Beholder 49
  - Alley Cat 50
  - HUSH 51
  - Dice of Life 52
  - Spineless 54
  - Sticks and Stones 55
  - Energy Channel 56
  - Zoetendal 57
  - War of the Words 58
  - Mind the Gap 60
  - STEM 61
  - Miners of the North 62
  - The Tablecloth 64
  - Rolling in the Mud 65
  - Idiosyncratic 66

BOUNCE BACK	67
Shattered	69
Relationship Redundancy	70
Fight or Flight	71
No Limits	72
Ice Queen	74
Bounce	75
Scuffed Shoes	76
Payback	77
Family Tree	78
Insomniac	79
Stark Portrait	80
Love Don't Hurt Me Anymore	82
Teacher's Pet	83
Defiant	84
The Sun on my Face	85
Tealeaves	86
Sail Away	87
Lightning Bolt	88
Blind Mice	89
Bleach	90
Padlock	92
Puppet-on-a-String	92
Foot Loose	93
Square Peg	94
Purify	96
Fighting the Current	97
The Skin I'm In	98
Ping Pong	99
Hosier Lane	100

Opposites Attract 102
RISE UP 103
   Reflect 105
   The Trumpet 106
   Three Minutes 107
   Hot Air Balloon 108
   Country Girl/Urban Boy 109
   Brick Wall 110
   Arrival Hall 111
   Away Song Bird 112
   Red or Dead 114
   An Ode to a Bully 115
   Housebound 116
   Animal King 'Dom' 118
   War 'Verses' Peace 120
   Step Back to Existence 121
   Rejoice 122
   Silver Lining 123
   Opportunity Knocks 124
   Working-class Lass 125
   Set Adrift 126
   Inimitable 127
   Compass North 128
   No Place Like Home 129
   The Gamble 130
   Ringmaster 131
   Spring Clean 132
   Affirmation 133
   Willpower 134
   Rise 135

- Subversive Epigrams 136
- **FLY HIGH** 139
  - Phantasmagoria 141
  - The Immigrant 142
  - Me, Myself and I 143
  - Smile 143
  - Nelson's Column 144
  - Growth Spurt 146
  - Pigtails 147
  - Musical Youth 148
  - One of a Kind 150
  - Street Art 151
  - Weeds 152
  - Success Elements 154
  - Turning the Tables 155
  - Va-Va-Voom 156
  - Dreams 157
  - Technophobia 158
  - Ambition of an Author 162
  - Roadblocks 163
  - Love between the Lines 164
  - Winning Game 164
  - On the Chin 165
  - Diamond in the Rough 166
  - Solitary Superstition 167
  - Days of Summer 168
  - Only You 169
  - Space Odyssey: Beyond Tomorrow 170
  - Encore! 172
  - Graffiti Lane 173

ACKNOWLEDGEMENTS... 175
ABOUT THE AUTHOR... 181

KICKED DOWN

PINK BUBBLES

Pink bubbles
pop up my nose
while swigging from glass bottle
cold on inexperienced lips
cheap sharpness on a tongue
growing alcohol tolerance to
mask growing pains

Teenage figures
blur before teary eyes
laughing across the park
one spraying sick graffiti
two smoking dope
rocking on the seesaw
uppers and downers

Lonely life
beneath the tree
slumped against rough bark
body blending with Mother Nature
mind grappling with the universe
soul adrift without roots
outcast and invisible

Pink bubbles
easier to swallow with every gulp
smoothing out the edges
balancing alone on a branch
like a bird with clipped wings
unable to migrate
trapped in a secluded nest

NETTLES

You make my skin itch
like a nettle sting I can't
stop scratching until

I bleed.

SMELL THE ROSES

When you closed the door without looking back
you must have known cruel sting of mother's palm
would leave marks on soft thighs of blue and black
always a storm before elusive calm

Face soaks pillow, soul drowning, body sore
breath shallow as lips purse in silent scream
balloon has popped, daddy's girl no more
icing on cake nothing more than ancient dream

Footsteps in passage, blood throbs inside vein
fear haemorrhaging from confused young heart
her scent is of roses as she raises cane
creating wounds that ache and smart

Arguments skirted, duties deserted
Why were your efforts to stay not concerted?

WHEN THE BELL TOLLS

The bell tolls three times
proclaiming to the office a sale has been attained
triggering a tsunami of celebrations
clapping
cheering
beneath breath
jealous jeering
at golden success of a colleague
conquering a mountain of unrealistic targets
relegating the rest of us into overshadowed shame
forcing us to commit terrible crimes
spitting in coffee
deleting important files
depleting confidence
until eventually
death of a salesman is inevitable

SWIPE

Aching thumb
fingers numb
from swiping smooth screen
streaking smart glass

Tweeting
Instagram bleating
working faster and faster
searching profiles

in a murky pond
desperate to extend the network and form a bond
reaching out to explore
virtual possibilities

Poking
some think I'm joking
just some sad stranger
trying to gather likes

Filling the blip
of lack of real friendship
even the bullying monkeys on my back
blocked me long ago

Log on and dive in
no messages to make me grin
cast my rod across the ocean spanning
six degrees of separation

attempting to catch a fish
on the hook
finding nothing but a one-dimensional
face in an online *book*

LOST DIAMOND

I
was
always
alone growing up,
deserted at birth by my mother,
a diamond who passed away too young, without knowing me.
At first my father tried his best
but too much of
a struggle
was
I

OBEY MY COMMAND

once a soldier of honour
a man in uniform standing proud
   shiny shoes
   shiny medals
   shiny weapon

once a soldier of war
fighting for an unknown cause
   don't ask questions
   don't have opinions
   don't disobey

once a soldier in formation
acting on instructions barked from above
   marched into the mess room
   marched into enemy territory
   marched into the arms of death

once a soldier alive on the frontline
now at peace as flag flies at half mast
   should have gone AWOL
   should have joined the navy
   should be forever remembered a hero

GREASED PALM

Tirades dished out, I chew on each slowly
    until they tattoo tongue
    unhealthy blue jelly bean stains to a child
    in the corner of a playground without slide

Creativity quashed; colourful post-it notes crushed while
    on receiving end of demeaning
    prefixing sarcasm
    I was only joking

Back in my box, can't think outside it since
    accused of false errors
    finger pointing at
    my cowering silence

I did check / please inspect / don't disrespect

Boss camouflaged beneath radar
    declaring fast-moving targets
    staring, glaring
    hostile enemy without gun

Who needs a Smith and Wesson?
    colossal grenades to throw
    duck and grin
    pretend it's fun

Ignore reports on performance
    crosses in every square
    itching to go home
    instead of suffering there

Work late / barely ate / still the hate

Meeting over, trundle past cubicles, make the coffee
> *two sugars, Sir, or three?*
> metal spoon stirs in my hand
> wooden spoon in his

Lightbulb back on
> mind maps, thought showers
> encouraged to innovate
> minutes drag into hours

Credit stolen, rug swiped from under feet
> *give Sir a bonus!*
> unanimous clap
> while I reel from the slap

His palm attracts the grease / keep the peace / no work police

Toss and turn between sheets
> a tryst with insomnia
> sun rises, shave the bristles
> a gauntlet to run

Camaraderie extinct, blood squeezed from a stone
> elbows on desk
> anxious head in feeble hands
> morale low, self-esteem blown

Tell myself what I've always known
> nefarious behaviour unacceptable
> yet unable to quit
> as I see fit

Despite the rage / can't turn the page / reliant on wage

CANDY FLOSS

we shared candy floss once at the fair
after spinning around on the Waltzer
until we were dizzy in the tunnel of love

we pulled crackers and wore paper hats
reading jokes after eating turkey with cranberry jelly
hysterical with full-belly laughs

we clambered to the top of Arthur's Seat
after seeing the Edinburgh Tattoo at the castle
bagpipes ringing in our ears as we held hands

we ate buttery croissants together in bed
crumbs gathering amongst rumpled sheets
you made us steaming hot coffee to wash them down

we cried salty tears together at the end
after the fighting overshadowed the love
my heart crushed as you closed the door softly behind you

WHAT MIGHT HAVE BEEN

pain is not knowing
when you will come home

regret is not knowing
what might have been had we not met

insanity is not knowing
what is real in the life that we share

heartache is not knowing
if I will ever get over you

GLASS HALF EMPTY

Topsy turvy, upside down
Turned my smile into a frown
Glass half empty, never half full
A car in trouble, push or pull
See you later, let's talk soon
Shooting stars fall as I aim for the moon

Umbrella goes up as rain pours down
Laughter epidemic caused by my tears of a clown
My roots sink low as other plants sprout tall
Dam levels rise, I'm drowning in the waterfall
A weird black bat hanging from a tree
Paying for mistakes when advice is free

Big bullies belittling folk
Hurting feelings, life's no joke
Verbal abuse, no physical pain
Inside my mind are four walls of insane
Mental health declines, suicide rates on the rise
When I jump, will eyebrows rise in surprise?

A life too short, insufferable depression too long
They pushed me to it, cruel words their song
No baby born, or couple wed
No celebration in my name, only a funeral for the dead
Lonely body buried, nobody to love
Will anyone pray for my resurrection to Heaven above?

DEFACED

Bruise
tender, sore
throbbing, smarting, hurting
bash, thump, punch, blow
maiming, harming, wounding
black, blue
Abuse

EGGSHELLS

Toss between sheets
Alone in the night
Evading sleep
Dreading dawn breaking

You arrive home for breakfast
Lipstick visible on collar
I recoil from the sickly scent
Of foreign perfume clinging to your skin

Turn my head from your guilty kiss
Duplicitous lips skim one cheek
Your wandering palm slaps the other
I make you bacon and eggs

I'm sick of over-easy
Stomach churns at your sunnyside up
Yolk trickling down your face
Tears streaming down mine

Wash the dishes
Suds keep my hands soft
Yours are hard enough for us both
Pull plug, watch dirty water slip away

Scrub the work surfaces
Eggshells fall to the floor
Sweep them away
No longer want to walk on them

You run the shower upstairs
I turn on the kitchen tap
Smirking as you scream
I'm in hot water, you shiver in cold

Kelly Van Nelson

Bags are packed, money stashed
Plan was to flee last night
Still here, brain scrambled
Like tomorrow's eggs

PLAY THE HAND

boot laces tied in knots match those forming in stomach
rifle a heavy boulder slung over shoulder
helmet protecting thoughts ricocheting inside head
from lethal bullets laying assault on their survival

tread daily path into the unknown field
battling with the chance of saving lives from nuclear war
versus odds of being blind-sighted by not-so-friendly fire

return to base with nothing but an empty hand
no WOMD buried in the sand

camaraderie as we eat tinned fruit
share illicit contents from hip flask
reminisce on home-cooked roast as we roast in the wicked heat

bunk down for forty winks
impossible to tune out snores from
twenty sleeping men selfishly grabbing theirs
good on 'em

pull open filing cabinet of memories
each a record of time spent with the love of my life
focus on the one pulling crackers with her last Christmas
before this tour left us craving only one present:
to be present

march back out on foot at the crack of dawn
check ground for evidence of land mines
stare towards rooftops for visuals of snipers
peek in doorways for signs of ambush
break out in a sweat
worrying about blowing up is making me crack up

Kelly Van Nelson

verbal abuse breaks out over
who has a cherry in their tinned fruit salad
flasks stay on the hip
stories decline into comparing notches on bedheads
fight breaks out over derogatory comment about my missus
first punch was mine

grab the night goggles
take the tank for midnight spin
streets are quiet
menacing and eerie

divide grows big enough to need the
graffitied West Bank barricade between us
half the squad want to lob a grenade
the rest want to pump lead into anything that moves

fear of dying of boredom overtakes fear of the enemy
someone will die of stupidity soon

cut my thumb clean off on tinned fruit lid
amputated tip shoved in empty hip flask
evacuated to medical for surgery
sewn back together
sent home for Christmas to pull a cracker
glad I played my hand at the right moment in the war

AQUA VITAE

Impartial to Scotch, prone to enjoying a few
Equally, connoisseur of a good Irish brew

Many a recipe distils it twice
Exception to rule, distil it thrice

'Tis the word of old Robbie Burns
Poet who drank while spouting eloquent words

St Patrick would claim the Irish founded it first
Potent drink to quench overwhelming thirst

Malt bolls produced from makers of repute
An invention of genius, one cannot dispute

Illicit poteen to avoid the tax fee
Whisky or Whiskey, spelt with an E

No matter origin: Speyside, Islay, or Cork
Angels' share evaporates from barrels of oak

Natural spring water, copper pot stills with a gleam
Talisker, Laphroig, Independent Colleen

Distilleries delivering the drink to the man
Proclaimed by bagpipes, the tunes of a clan

In Latin, for centuries, called Aqua vitae
The water of life for you and for I

A dash or a dram, a nip or a tot
A bottle, a double, a conservative shot

Cheers to friends, near and afar
Who share passion for Whiskey in the Jar

Golden liquid that consumes every second of thought
Tormenting weak fools to drink more than they ought

A coin of two faces; best friend or foe
Fills body with delight, leaves soul empty with woe

Graffiti Lane

NIGHT TERRORS

demons
create terror
stirring anxious feelings
through constant tormenting from the
devil

Kelly Van Nelson

DINNER FOR ONE

I remember the angst of scavenging for nourishment;
the excitement when sustenance
was found in a tin of corned beef
selected from the self-service menu in a kitchen
where stony silence
and the acrid smell of burned baked beans
lingered in the air.

My parched lips washed it down
with unfiltered tap water
consumed while perched on a rickety chair
that wobbled as if laughing at my misfortune.

The chipped orphan plate in front of my hungry eyes
was a pleasure to behold,
the pièce de résistance on scratched pine surface
barren of pretty tablecloth.

Indigestion took hostage of my stomach
when I too quickly shovelled
morsels into my young mouth
using any utensil other than a silver spoon.

It was cold in the bosom of the kitchen
without the oven on.

CORPORAL PUNISHMENT

Caned my palms for failing to listen
to your psalms performed; blood made them glisten

DOG DAYS ARE OVER

Enclosed behind glass like a jewel in a museum,
faces pressed at the window, eyes roam over me.
My wrinkles sag, hair too short to stand on end,
nubbin tail with no wag as humans walk on instead.

Eventually, I'm relocated to a new home
on a corner block next to a two-storey mansion.
My wooden pad not as flash: one tiny room, no front door,
sparse furnishings, a rough blanket decorating the floor.

On occasion, invited inside for vigorous scrub behind ears,
under armpits, around eyes. Growl and shake –
at least they reward my perpetual frown with uncooked steak;
I'd prefer well-done but swallow down.

I pay my rent by doing gardening jobs: digging holes,
burying rubbish like old smelly bones.
Hard labour is tiring. 'Let me rest,' I bark,
yet my new owners drag me on leash to the park.

This English Bully's dog days are over.

KER PLUNK

Marble balancing on fragile sticks
Every move I make threatening
To topple over our relationship

Think carefully before I bring it all
Tumbling down around us

Everything I touch has an irreversible effect
On you and our children
The fragile glass in my life

When I resolve to pull the pin
It will be game over
I have to be sure

REPUDIATED MIRACLE

My child, he is an angel
Ingrained goodness, clear as glass
A smile to melt a hardened heart
Features carved into an art

My child, he throbs with joy
Innocence pure and sweet
A hand in mine, clutching life
The reason husband takes a wife

Each moment golden treasure
Diamonds rough and smooth
Asleep I see him in my dreams
Awake my pain is wrenched to screams

Sorrow, my blanket of darkness
Anger coursing my veins
The Lord, illness delivered
Left him enervated, withered

My child, he is an angel
His breath, a whisper vanished
I pummelled, pleaded, remonstrated
A miracle, He repudiated

First Published in Poetry by Moonlight, 2009 by UK Poetry Society Ltd

TIGHT SPOT

Spot of bother since
leopard never changes spots.
Need ladybird luck.

THE TUXEDO PRINCESS

A bright new era for The Tuxedo Princess
Staff in naval uniforms, patrons dressed to impress
Anchored in Tyneside, a nightclub of fame
Majestic vessel of grandiose steel

Majestic vessel of grandiose steel
Decades of dance music, consuming the soul
Walk the plank to the revolving dance floor
Bodies vying for attention, south bank attraction

Bodies vying for attention, south bank attraction
New nightclubs spawning a breeding ground
Press reported refurbishment costing unaffordable pound
'The Boat', once proud, a crumbling facade

'The Boat', once proud, a crumbling facade
Afloat, an island, her gangway amputated
Water lapping sides, mocking in movement
Moored in ghostly silence, desolate in death

Moored in ghostly silence, desolate in death
Final fate, towed for scrap: journey over troubled water
Quayside of commerce, a river now clean
North East improving, tourist money to glean

North East improving, tourist money to glean
Council bulldozing: lay red carpet fit for queen
Wrinkled royalty once adrift, denied her facelift
No bright new era for The Tuxedo Princess

Graffiti Lane

NEW KID ON THE BLOCK

Friend
I miss you
Since moving away
Now the new kid on the block
Hanging on the street corner
Alone after school
Write to me
Friend

MIRROR, MIRROR ...

Some days he loves me
Others he loves me not
Some nights he's tender
When he hasn't drunk a shot

Some days he's charming
When others are around
Some nights he's alarming
I try not to make a sound

Some days I want to leave him
Escape to pastures greener
Some days I think I'm lucky
Maybe other men are meaner

Some days my hands shake
I steady them with a drink
Some days I clear the bottle
It helps me not to think

Some days I feel so angry
That all I do is shout
Some days I raise my hand
When my kid's acting the lout

Some days in the mirror
The face is weary, grim
Some days staring back
The reflection is of him

DID HE KNOW?

Did he know
the sun would never rise
without his daughter
thinking of being tickled
under the armpits,
tickled pink at having a daddy at home
like all her friends at school?

When he divorced her mother
did he know
the sun would never set
without her crying herself to sleep,
leaving the pillow
soaked with despair?

After a week passed by
of her breath
making clouds on the window
as she waited in vain
for him to stroll up the garden path,
her stomach churning from famine,
desperately craving the nourishing sound
of the doorbell ringing,
did he know
the simple things would become difficult:
laughing, dancing, singing?

On the day she graduated from college
decorated with distinction,
did he know
how worthless she felt
to have nobody there
congratulating her?
Was it conceited
to want to shine in the limelight
and see it reflected
in a proud father's eyes?

During moments of self-destruction,
when pity's poison ivy
spawned around her neck
and confusion wrapped its lead weight
around her ankles,
did he know
vile names manifested inside her skull,
tormenting her with relentless verbal abuse –
defenceless, unlovable, rejected nuisance?

That heartbreaking moment when she received news
from a distant relative
of the funeral he starred in last year,
did he know
how peace might be with him
but would evade her until the day
she joined him in Heaven
to demand answers?

SNAKE CHARMER

charmer
slithers past
a reptile in the grass
darting sharp tongue
shedding skin
yet never morphing
always a poisonous
snake

THE JESTER

Corners of the mouth turned up in smile
Eyes crinkled in laughter
Master of the masquerade
You had us all fooled

Despair overcome quickly
Self-inflicted quips about hardships befallen on you
Humour used as a defence
We didn't see the attack you were battling alone

Medication controlling emotions
Keeping erratic behaviour in check
Rattling inside your stomach, never digesting
Sickness hidden behind colourful costume

Depression finally diagnosed
We gave you an overdose of love
Daily phone calls, weekly coffee, monthly therapy
You gave us an overdose back

Calendar full of events
Retrospectively marked with a red cross
Tomorrow the day is empty
Nothing to check off since you checked out

♯

when I tagged the New York subway
didn't know I'd end up with a tag on the leg
tagged a criminal
#graffiti

SPEAK OUT

FACELESS WITHOUT ART

turn down the darkest alley
spiders scuttling for shelter behind rancid bins
at the sound of footsteps

breath steams up behind
handkerchief tied across moist mouth

bricks crying out for decoration
to stand out from the crowd
craving distinction

just like me without my art
they are nothing but a bland background

rattle the can and spray
in a burst of energy
matched with the rush in my gut

meticulous in executing design
never to be confused with trash

stand back and admire handiwork
surge of pride from stepping up the originality stakes
this statement will make people stop and stare in delight

pack up the paint and expose the face
i'm a nobody again

Graffiti Lane

BULLY 'FOUR' YOU

You bully me –
bully 'four' *you*.
You know this
says more about
you than me?

SPARKLE

A magpie
swoops from the tree,
wings flapping as I mirror the movement,
vigorously shaking my arms.

The physical attack is not because I sparkle
but because she does
as she protects her offspring
during mating season.

Not everything is as black and white as
a magpie.

DIVERSITY

Domination of corporate giants by men in pinstripe suits
   Investment in female talent falls below funding annual golf day
      Vent frustration at the injustice
         Encourage open-minded approach to balancing the scales
            Rage builds beneath starched white collars at my insolence
               Stand my ground
                  It's time for change
                     Today not tomorrow
                        Yes to diversity

BIG BULLIES, SMALL MINDS

big bullies impose
feeble attempts to exert
control over you

small minds crave power
attempting to manufacture your
insecurities

brave hearts know strength grows
from revelling in being
unique – being you

TALK BACK

An argument,
when one-sided,
is an oppressive,
dictated opinion.

INSIDE OUT

Better to be bullied and learn to survive
than to be the bully and be dead inside.

THE WHISTLEBLOWER

Nurse wheels the bed into cubicle
      sides up to prevent occupant rolling
      onto disinfected floor
      in a bundle of frail bones and wrinkled skin

Contraption cages dying elderly patient
      mummified between starched sheets
      hospital corners perfected
      by efficient nurse with strained angelic pout on thin lips
      eyes void of animation

She does the rounds
      checking shiny fob
      jotting notes on clipboard
      stored at foot of bed
      habitual clicking of retractable pen
      every time she moves to a new patient

Vitals are checked by cold, callused hands
      blood pressure monitored by the sour-faced nurse
      deficient of concern as she records
      exceptionally high temperature

Pills rattle in container
      two in my dose ...
      usually

Today she dispenses an orphan capsule
      served with a glass of water
      washed down with a steely stare

Kelly Van Nelson

Hand disfigured with subcutaneous infusion wire
       shakes as it accepts the proffered gift
       eyes filling with tears before lids droop
       and memories cloud

Sun is shining into cubicle as I wake
       to feel the pain of fresh black and blue intrusions

TV hanging above bed on bracket is on mute
       subtitles reporting news of 'whistleblower' coming forward
       spouting tales of woe about a hospice
       where patients are physically abused

Nurse is centre screen
       a heroine with familiar strained angelic pout

The 'whistleblower' marred my skin and stole my medicine
       but I'm as mute as the TV
       unable to speak out

AGAINST ALL ODDS

All she desired was to be allowed to learn
For girls to be granted an education
Instead they marched her to the stake to burn

Sentenced to death by brutal assassination
For speaking out for basic human rights
Shot in the head by the Taliban

Terrorists thought they could silence her plea
Put a stop to the freedom of speech
Cut the head off ambition

Instead they fed the belly of hope
An insurgence of women brimming with courage
Not afraid of fighting extremists with pen and pencil

A miracle survivor against all odds
Winner of the Nobel Peace Prize
She is Malala

Kelly Van Nelson

THROUGH THE EYES OF THE BEHOLDER

tin cans crushed into modern sculptures
plastic bags made into bead bracelets
murals sprayed on bland brick walls
#artorvandalism

Graffiti Lane

ALLEY CAT

Leave the pub, walk home, clip-clap
Dark night, quiet street, don't look back

Footsteps creep up, close behind
Glance back – nothing, flying blind

Breath down neck, I start to run
Pushed down alley, glinting gun

Cat-claw defence, slap, clip-clap
Scream out and run, don't look back!

HUSH

HUSH little baby
Don't say a word
Your beauty whispers sweet nothings
From the wall where you perch

Atop street art ladder
HUSH layers divergent colour palette
Blending old and new cultures
Rejoiced by Geordie talent

Memoirs of a geisha
Sensuous female form
HUSH modern graffiti
Creates immortal storm

Hidden Asian eyes
Kanzashi decorates jet black hair
Brick by brick
HUSH paints your legacy there

DICE OF LIFE

Waiting, tick-tock,
Doc is on the clock.

The queue snakes long and thin
preparing to shed obsolete layer of old skin,
sheathing hissing people from all walks of life,
inking enough hospital admission paperwork to fell a tree
even though Wi-Fi is free.

Healthcare technology modernisation didn't warrant
triple digit dial-in rights
with an ambulance escort powered by flashing blue lights.

What's the emergency? No rush
to digitise the filing cabinet crush.

Patients – some lucky like me –
relish four walls of privileged privacy,
maxing out the medical fund,
minimising flimsy curtain exposure,
bumping the list
rather than lingering so long body develops a cyst
while crawling to the top of the government schedule
as ailments prevail:
aches and pains of joints, back, neck, nose, throat –
if one's lucky, no organs of note.

Surgery demand is a virus rife,
punters rolling the dice of life,
placing the chip on black or red,
hoping to avoid winding up dead.

Checked in, scrubbed down, gowned up,
anaesthetic wipes me out.

Kelly Van Nelson

No time to protest
after results of merciless last test.

Oncologist, gastroenterologist, neurologist,
radiologist, cardiologist, rheumatologist,
immunologist, dermatologist, endocrinologist,
haematologist, nephrologist, otolaryngologist,
pathologist, pulmonologist and urologist;
it's nothing but a wish list –
any would be better than this
intrusion by the gynaecologist
digging down there like an archaeologist.

Bleep. F**k. Bleep. F**k.
Bruised and stitched when I wake up.

Cup of tea, cup of pee,
blood pressure dip, back on the drip,
swallow the med, ham sandwich on bread,
feet feel cold, body feels old,
mind distorted, nurse report it!

"Remember your name?
Hope we don't see you again,
sorry to bully, staff in a hurry,
call your lift, cut wrist band off
before the end of day shift."

Waiting, tick-tock,
Doc is on the clock.

Shortlisted 2018 in UK flash contest by Retreat West and published in 2019 in Reflex Fiction by Reflex Press

Graffiti Lane

SPINELESS

malice
hurting others
with intentional digs
meanness beyond comprehension
spineless

STICKS AND STONES

Verbal sticks and
demeaning stones
tossed my way
can't break my bones.

Instead they crush
sensitive soul
into the pavement,
'twas mean-girl's goal.

Stomped between cracks,
chewed up gum,
nothing more than
a nuisance –
you done?

ENERGY CHANNEL

Fire burns bright
Channel into verse I write

Douse the scorch
Shine the torch

Kicked down
Constant frown

Bounce back
Don't wallow in black

Rise up
Fill the cup

Fly high
Truth not lies

Can't let rage
Consume the page

English plain
Graffiti Lane

ZOETENDAL

I am your accident,
a small vessel bobbing along merrily
until smashed against jagged rocks beneath the ocean
like the Zoetendal, run aground in Struisbaai.

I am your shipwreck
damaged in stormy weather,
body rusty from exposure to brutal elements,
head peeking above the waves at low tide.

I am your history,
part of your past, never to be forgotten,
gone from your future forever,
never to sail into your dangerous territory again.

I am your nemesis,
the reason a red and white lighthouse stands in L'Agulhas
warning of two oceans clashing on the southernmost tip of Africa,
shining the brightest beacon to guide other lost souls to safety.

WAR OF THE WORDS

Words: weapons of mass destruction, harmless when dormant underground, explosive when unleashed onto innocent lives, a bystander minding own business, trying to hide in the trenches from conflict, afraid to lift head for fear of battered helmet being incapable of withstanding a strike from a flying bullet. The scholarly head it protects is already down and out, wounded and weak, despondent from complaints made about the bully who uses weapons of mass destruction falling on deaf ears for too long due to lack of hard evidence. The spotlight is only now being shone on the situation, stemming from concerned public who petitioned for action to conserve the wellbeing of younger generations trying to navigate society, lest a blind eye would still be turned on such matters.

I'm dishing out tactics in generous rations, trying to make it interesting for my audience even though I know nothing of the frontline and never had to face an enemy who uses such underhand techniques to wear down resilience – I've been sitting behind a wooden desk barricade for thirty years, strategising about leadership techniques, analysing notable battles of history, teaching geography and speculating about the next country to launch into combat. My job today is to give these kids a plan of attack; to empower oneself to take ownership of the unruly situation, assert an aura of fight rather than flight, squeeze scarred body into Kevlar and face the enemy. This comes after my first instructions were not followed to the letter, so failed to protect the defenceless target. The sniper was ordered to stand down, but instead they put the eye piece on and zoomed in on landing the perfect next shot – a true marksman.

This undecorated sergeant rises to weary feet, chalking one more piece of free advice for the whole platoon to digest on the blackboard. A technique plagiarised from the British Army, an institution of long-standing honour that carries the wounded on shoulders rather than crush them underfoot, uncompromisingly gallant in the most treacherous situations. The radical method introduced by the British is aimed at rallying the troops on the sidelines; the bystander with gun in holster and knife in sheath whose indifference shows tacit consent to the aggressive use of a hand grenade of bullying words being tossed in civil war, causing irrefutable damage to the psyche of the recipient whose feet it lands at. Hope they can read my handwriting – left-handed teachers are just as messy as left-handed pupils. My latest command is scrawled, white on black:

The behaviour you walk past is the behaviour you condone.

The platoon reads these words in silence. One disrupter in the front row sniggers before I wipe the blackboard clean and the bell rings to dismiss my senior student class to go forth and gorge on Eaton Mess.

remunerate
increasing pay grade
rewarding men for
invisible discretionary effort
on top of clocked time
forever in their prime

MIND THE GAP

gender salary gap
thirst quenched by leaky tap
drip, drip, drip
women spending a lifetime
trying to amend
historical trend

STEM

Scientific virtuoso men in white lab coats
   Technology testosterone
      Engineering Eureka!
         Male mathematical prodigies

            STEM cell research

Simple to attract XY chromosomes
   To dominate the physical world
      Executing disproportionate control over nature
      Must increase XX students to diversify in

              STEM education

MINERS OF THE NORTH

Black sedimentary rocks create sizzling flares,
fossil fuel combusting akin to illicit affairs,
blasting out coal, satisfying political desire,
earth's minerals giving origin to fire.
A flourishing period, lifelong friendships morph
between unsung heroes, coal miners of the north.

Navigating tunnels through bleak underground cavern,
faces surface, gulp air, before propping up tavern.
Fingernails filthy, pores clogged with sweat,
black lung disease chronic – lest we forget.
Masses bullied by unions, dogged with remorse
into pickets of unsung heroes, coal miners of the north.

Depressed in the darkness, deprived of the sun,
men afraid and confused, fighting with no gun.
Voices passionate for what they believe:
better conditions and working-class poverty reprieve.
Paparazzi emerge, hungry piranhas report
dirt on unsung heroes, coal miners of the north.

Steadfast in cabinet, the infamous Iron Lady,
no procrastination, not even a maybe.
Site closures from judge trigger-happy with mallet,
unemployment rises, deaf ears, where's the ballot?
Thousands gather in picket line cohort,
crowds of unsung heroes, coal miners of the north.

Rejected, dejected, united they stand,
illegal strikers depressed, shunned their demand.
Dust settles, mines abandoned, only scabs graft alone,
ice gripping hearts, chills consuming the home.
Empty hands defeated, voices mute of retort,
silenced unsung heroes, coal miners of the north.

Kelly Van Nelson

Stock exchange haemorrhaging, unemployment rife,
family arteries ruptured causing trouble and strife.
Young men of kindred spirit lucky to grow old,
big dreams crushed underfoot, their tale must be told.
Legends buried deep in core, renewable energies thrust forth,
nobody recalls the unsung heroes, coal miners of the north.

The past is long gone but history stays
forever in memories, told in yarns, films and plays,
reminding us all of the men below ground
who once became lost but now they are found
above the surface where sunlight shines,
a spotlight on the darkness that once was the mines.

They dug deep and fought for conditions valiantly sought.
We will never forget the coal miners of the north.

THE TABLECLOTH

Relaxing on the sands of
Melkbosstrand

Face upturned to the rays of the harsh
South African sun

Behind in the dunes, rustling from the dry depths of
Euphorbiaceae bushes

Filled with milky latex substance giving meaning to coastal suburb
Melkbos

Pronking in for a fleeting appearance is the native
Springbok

Focus drifts to kite surfers taming the wild
Atlantic Ocean

Framed by the craggy backdrop of majestic
Table Mountain

Clouds drift over, shrouding the table top with a pristine white
tablecloth

In the corner of my eye, the home for so long of Madiba
Robben Island

Body tenses, reminded of oppression and institutionalised segregation
Apartheid

The sand is soft under the weight on my shoulders on
Melkbosstrand

Kelly Van Nelson

ROLLING IN THE MUD

stand at front of room
poker faces staring back
shaking hand clicks on projector
dive into PowerPoint pack

go through analysed data
women's performance underrated
men in the room comment
facts are unsubstantiated

square shoulders, hold head high
confidently state my case
addressing the gender pay gap
requesting fairness for the human race

sneering from a peer
accusing me of talking sh*t
feel my cheeks burn bright
when told to get over it

automatically flex claws
anger boiling in my blood
I stop myself from biting back
with an emotional flood

if you roll in the mud
with a pig you'll get dirty
I keep my cool, stay on track
don't allow myself to get shirty

at presentation's end
I watch my boss stand
elated as he strolls to front
and shakes my shaking hand

IDIOSYNCRATIC

If we are all unique
we are all the same

If we are all the same
I want to be unique

BOUNCE BACK

SHATTERED

what once broke me
into a million pieces
is what now makes me
razor sharp

RELATIONSHIP REDUNDANCY

recruited to fill your needs
meet your predefined criteria
perfect talent match
best candidate for the job

worked like a slave
cleaning up after you
pandering to your every whim
always saying yes

tasks threw my way grew in complexity
unable to deliver to your expectations
on the receiving end of brutal
performance management techniques

skills have become obsolete
superfluous to requirements
replaced with a younger model
far more compliant than I've become

my role in your life is redundant
retired from service
under a severance agreement
time to check the small print for the payout

FIGHT OR FLIGHT

Swipe right
Turns to lust
Lust turns to love
Love turns to like
Like turns to fight
Fight turns to flight
I know you're not right
Swipe left on you tonight
Swipe right

No Limits

standing on cliff
arms spread wide
an angel on the edge

gully below
an expanse
of rocky terrain

brain commits
to the task
body refuses

impossible to step
into the abyss
senses scream in refute

mind over matter
this is my time
to push limits

been shackled so long
don't look back
in anger

take leap of faith
free-fall
tumble head over heels

gasp in shock
eyes bulging
regret my stupidity

blood rush to the head
jerk tugs me up
relief at the bounce

bungy jumping
is not for
the faint-hearted

ICE QUEEN

Blood was warm of baby born
but life squeezed tiny heart, turning veins
icy blue.

Above the surface calm and serene
showing select few dimensions –
iceberg.

Built walls thicker than an igloo.
Living alone inside a dome –
icehouse.

Gradually growing sharp-edged spikes,
forming stalagmites and stalactites –
icicles.

Blocked out all the hardship and pain
with a steely resilience –
ice-queen.

Blinded by the blizzard, bitter
until the sun warms the soul and
the ice melts.

BOUNCE

Kick me down, I bounce back up –
ignoring fissure damage cracking crustacean shell,
revealing concealed pearl rather than empty void.

Mindset is mine, not yours to take –
clinging to inner strength, rendering you unable to prise this
barnacle from the most jagged of rocks.

Scarred and marred, I bounce back up –
flourishing under the surface while you cause ripples above,
unable to anchor me down while trying to haul yourself up.

Soft flesh is mine, not yours to take –
eluding bite from jaws wide, poised ready for the kill
of weaker prey than me.

Your words fall flat, I bounce back up –
catching air; a soaring dolphin
never staying in the depths of the abyss too long.

The dream is mine, not yours to take –
to awaken and live life to its fullest while you toss and turn,
disturbed by whatever sea creature lurks under your own sea bed.

SCUFFED SHOES

Elbow in the ribs
hurts pride and bruises smooth skin
beneath faded school

blazer with frayed cuffs.
Hand-me-downs suck for poor third
invisible child

who hangs head during
recess to avoid trouble.
I once stood in those

scuffed lace-ups, feeling
ridiculed until Dad scored
new cushy job. Phew!

Inclusion's easy
for kids with money. 'Hello,'
I say. She smiles back.

PAYBACK

revenge is sweet
when it's sugar coated in
alimony

FAMILY TREE

Laughter fills the room
No longer at my expense
I smile in celebration

Family gathers together
Adopted since my originals are gone
Laughter fills the room

Jokes and jibes are shared
All in good taste
No longer at my expense

Heart opens to becoming a branch
On this deeply-rooted tree
I smile in celebration

Kelly Van Nelson

INSOMNIAC

Inadvertently hooked on your devilish charm
Nicotine in a cup
Smell, invisible as an airborne virus, fills my nostrils
Occupies my every thought
Makes my heart race
Never letting me sleep peacefully
Iron fist grips me, controlling my world
Adrenaline rush too addictive to quit
Coffee, milk, no sugar – I'm sweet enough

STARK PORTRAIT

Grainy image of a child
Barefoot in a street
Lined with council houses
Clothes ragged
Face dirty

Instant Polaroid of a teenage girl
Hair sprayed stiff in a quiff
Lipstick painted on forced smile
Glittering eyeshadow decorates
Shutters over sad stare

Glossy 6x4 of a YA
Backpack on lush grass
Thumbs up
Grinning on the edge of a lake
Surrounded by mountains

B&W stark portrait of a sophisticated model
Beautifully airbrushed
Reading *The New Yorker*
Surrounded by skyscrapers
Artistic and moody

Digital close-up of a woman
Baby in one arm
Other arm disappearing out of frame
Holding selfie stick
Left of centre

Bright family snap with filtered colours
Pop!
Sitting on the sand
Turquoise ocean in the distance
So blue it's too good to be true

Grainy image of a child
Deeply imprinted on the mother's mind
Chronicling the past
Casting unwanted shadow over the present
Sculpting the future

LOVE DON'T HURT ME ANYMORE

Hit
song plays
in my ears
obstructing thoughts
of the darker days
when charm blind-sided me.

Music makes me start to dance
in celebration of freedom
because I threw you out when your punch
drew blood and you sobbed, 'Sorry. I Love You!'

TEACHER'S PET

Sitting in the front row
furiously scribbling
answers to every question

Ruler hits the back of my head
I turn to see the culprit lower
his eyes to blank page

Teacher marks our papers
A+ on mine
D on yours

Next year I'll transition to a new front row of my choosing
while you are still here
left behind

I'll have rubbed you out of my life
There's no eraser for your grades

DEFIANT

Black
    silk
        fabric in rumpled heap on the floor

Black
    bruise
        beneath, tender and sore

Black
    eye
        showing the world what you've done

Black
    is your heart
        this time I will run

THE SUN ON MY FACE

born in a land ruled by regime
oppressed and distressed
face never allowed to be seen

flee to survive as buildings crumble
head low to avoid eye contact
bombs falling with loud rumble

cross the border by stealth
ostracised by new society
afraid I'm eating into home-grown wealth

enjoy the simple pleasure of sun on bare face
keep myself to myself
forgive but can't forget cruelty of the human race

open a shop selling the food of my childhood
a customer smiles at me every day
makes me his wife – I celebrate motherhood

my family now an integral part of the community
laughter fills our home
in this land filled with opportunity

TEALEAVES

Cup of English tea
treats ailments better than what
the doctor ordered

SAIL AWAY

Yesterday, I was a child, carefree and young
Today, a lost teenager, frayed lace comes undone
Tomorrow, I hope for the opportunity to flee

Yesterday, I crayoned colours outside the lines
Today, everyone judges, issuing vindictive fines
Tomorrow, I hope they hear my plea

Yesterday, I was cuddled, swaddled in cotton wool
Today, everyone sniggers, treating me like a fool
Tomorrow, I hope eyes open and see

Yesterday, I was blinded by Easter Bunnies, Santa Claus
Today, I am winded; give yourselves a round of applause
Tomorrow, I hope wind catches my sails, steering to sea

Yesterday, I was in kindergarten; any tears were brief
Today, kids are hurtful, throwing buckets filled with grief
Tomorrow, I'm going to live and be free

LIGHTNING BOLT

Thunder rumbles
Dark and depressed
Time for a new start
Lightning strikes

BLIND MICE

The cat's claws are out
Scratching at the weakest prey
Three blind mice, see how they run

Bored cat needs new prey
What better than the unsuspecting
Two blind mice, see how they run

Didn't see the cat
No witness to the attack
One blind mouse, see how you run

The blind can now see
Three mice together stand free
From one lonely cat

BLEACH

Blonde hair, curly, wild, free of products
manufactured to tame the mane.
Eyebrows so pale they fade into my pallid skin.
Freckles refuse to make an appearance
in harsh northern weather.
Bleach, the mean-girls crow during recess.
If they dare step close enough, they might see
something etched in this otherwise featureless face –
Defiant Girl.

Makeup is cheap for shoplifters from low-income families.
Easy to slip cherry-blossom lipstick down elastic waistband;
a quadrant of glittering eyeshadow under tight AA bra strap.
Hot property is all the rage at school.
Everybody does it; only the stupid get caught.
The Old Bill would be lenient on a first-time offender like me
yet I keep my hands tucked in pockets –
Good Girl.

Peer pressure from all angles to cake my face;
harassed by elbows digging into my sides
as we spill from class into the halls.
Bleach. Bleach. Bleach.
The chant is a ritual from witches trying to cast a spell
potent enough to break me.
To turn me into a pretty mannequin.
To make tears gush from dead eyes.
If they succeed, a fringe benefit of
no mascara is no streaks…
but they don't –
Unwavering Girl.

Each morning I dive out of bed, raring to learn:
English. Science. Geography. Maths.

     A   =   1
   grade   way ticket

to anywhere other than here.
The world has much to offer, but first I must
endure detention (maybe suspension),
after main tormentor receives fist in face
just before badminton practice.
Retaliation lowers me to her standard –
Bad Girl.

Her eye turns a shade of purple.
My cheeks abandon red angry blotches,
returning to unblemished, pale complexion.
Bleach. Bleach. Bleach.
Headmaster demands we apologise to one another.
Head bowed, she mumbles,
Sorry.
Head high, I retaliate loud and clear,
Sorry.
Hard not to feel satisfied for finally taking her to town.
Chair scrapes as I stand tall –
Liberated Girl.

I walked out and
never looked back.
Didn't need to,
nobody was on my back –
Big Girl.

Graffiti Lane

PADLOCK

When we first met you discovered
      the combination to open me up

I provided you with a key that gave you permission
      to come and go in my life as you pleased

You locked me up tight
      taking away my freedom

It's time to change the combination
      to something only I know

PUPPET-ON-A-STRING

      Punch
      in the gut
      as I walk away,
yet I know it's for the best –
    I was your puppet
      on a string;
        Judy

Kelly Van Nelson

FOOT LOOSE

footprints cross the threshold
newlyweds enjoying first steps together

downtrodden from unprovoked kicks
from a boot with steel caps

shackled feet rooted to black spot
unable to walk away from the torment

shoes in the bottom of a suitcase
packed with essentials to run

bare feet in soft sand
freedom trickling between toes

SQUARE PEG

Innocence lost and wisdom found
    True love, it hit me hard
Square peg in hole round
    Pierced heart with sharpest shard

Filled my days, consumed the night
    Enjoyed no longer living alone
Until the anger caused a fight
    Chilled me to the bone

I raised the bar, you raised your hand
    And brought it down in rage
Buried my head beneath the sand
    Scared to turn the page

To all the world, we hid it well
    Though smiles never reached my eyes
Looked the part, no kiss and tell
    In hindsight most unwise

You broke a bone and broke my heart
    Neither a first-time offence
Awarded you with another fresh start
    No self-confidence

For way too long, I felt the shame
    Until one day I snapped
No longer would I take the blame
    Time you went and packed

Quite a scene was caused the day
    I tossed you on the street
A hand wrapped round my hoarse throat
    Force knocked me off my feet

Kelly Van Nelson

You kicked me down, I bounced back up
    Called police to come around
Locked you away, I raise my cup to
    Innocence lost and wisdom found

Graffiti Lane

PURIFY

Water under bridge,
washing away the darkness.
Summer showers cleanse.

FIGHTING THE CURRENT

mesmerised
by unwavering stare
deeper than the abyss of ocean

occupied
with the love of my life
drifting apart from friends and family

conditioned
to be seen but not heard
deafening waves crashing in my ears

struggling
against the riptide
finding the strength to swim ashore

Do I look fat in this?
Should I die my hair?
How old do I look?
Am I not good enough for you?

THE SKIN I'M IN

I'm comfortable in my skin,
I prefer the natural look.
Age is but a number.
You love me just the way I am.

Kelly Van Nelson

PING PONG

Messing with lives is not a sport
Using others' downfalls to gloat
Relish the game, winning straight set
Ping Pong, bouncing over the net

Strive for the point, nothing held back
You hit out and give me a whack
No time at all to get upset
Ping Pong, bouncing over the net

Game, set, and match, I fist pump air
No care for tournament unfair
I walk off court with no regret
Ping Pong, bouncing over the net

HOSIER LANE

stroll down Hosier Lane
grab aromatic coffee from vendor killing it from miniscule premises
furnished with rickety antiques

cobblestones beneath my heels
paving the way for Melbourne pedestrians
walking about their business

hustle and bustle in every direction
as the sun shines brightly on the alley
and its eclectic inhabitants

after a late night at the office
retrace my footsteps along the glistening wet path
as the rain drizzles and dusk settles in

shutters conceal every shop front
traders absent, already cashed in for the day
the sound of traffic humming in the distance

a lone figure looms ahead
hunched over, hoodie tugged over head
mouth masked by black bandana

the distance between us shortens
my breath quickens in anticipation
of the unknown

his work is breathtaking:
a man in dreadlocks playing a didgeridoo
spray painted in bright colours beneath iron window bars

I nod in acknowledgement
the street artist continues his masterpiece
as the rain begins to clear

Kelly Van Nelson

at the top of Hosier, I glance back at the iconic graffiti zone
an evolving canvas for expressive creativity to flourish
beautiful, bright, bold

OPPOSITES ATTRACT

I love you to the moon and back
You love too many others

I pray each day for happiness
You pray each night for money

I laugh at jokes few and far between
You laugh right in my face

I pull my hair into the latest styles
You pull out my hair in fists

I pack my bags in secret
You pack a rotten punch

I drink a toast the day I leave
You drink your life away alone

RISE UP

                                    Rise up
            you are beautiful inside and outside
                      sing happily and dance
                         today and tomorrow
         choose friends wisely and unequivocally
                 laugh loudly and always smile
                            concede gracefully
                                 surf and swim
                                   always grow
                   sleep peacefully and deeply
                              dream frequently
                               love and cherish

REFLECT

cherish and love
frequently dream
deeply and peacefully sleep
grow always
swim and surf
gracefully concede
smile always and loudly laugh
unequivocally and wisely friends choose
tomorrow and today
dance and happily sing
outside and inside beautiful are you
Up rise

THE TRUMPET

Harsh frost hardens earth,
oppressor of growth and life.
Winter's wrath.

Peeking above ground,
yellow head catching first light.
Daffodil's petals.

Blowing loud trumpet,
a new tune singing brightly.
Announcing spring.

THREE MINUTES

Three minutes – blood, sweat, tears
sliding down bruised face of
determined boxer

Light on feet, dancing
centre of floor until crash
on ropes – featherweight

Boundless energy
to knock out opponent in
combat with fair punch

Two steel wills battle
for gold champion's belt.
Tears, sweat, blood – three minutes

HOT AIR BALLOON

Every time you put me down
it gave me a power boost to

rise

You dispensed the hot air

that made me fly

COUNTRY GIRL/URBAN BOY

straw in golden hair
red dust coating worn boots
good country girl
always true to her roots
never did she tire of
sunsets to the west
on the horizon
a bright orange zest
booked a girl's impromptu trip
for Mojitos to flow
on the edge of the Yarra
then the laneways they go
stumbling into mysterious
man in a mask
who gave her a stare
robbed her breath with a gasp   spray can in hand
urban artist and she destined   handkerchief over face
to marry one day   bad city boy
serendipity was always   never cared for the chase
going to have her wicked way   liked to sleep late
                                     skip sunrise on the east
                             no lovers destined to cross
                  never the twain distractions shall meet
                                  at dusk as the shutters
                             pulled down on the trade
                               he liked to use stencils
                          create statements on parade
                                  graffiti was his life
                          until the day that she walked
                                up Duckboard Place
                          this girl stopped and talked
         admiring his work with a dimple and smile
                              one day he was painting
                       the next waltzed up the aisle

BRICK WALL

When I turned down a dark lane
you took my hand and guided me in another direction

When four walls closed in on me
you told me to look up and see the stars and the moon

When there was a pile of bricks blocking my path
you made me believe I could climb over to the other side

When my path ahead was unclear amidst a maze of options
you held my hand as we got lost together

When I lay curled in a ball on the cold ground
you picked me up and helped me focus on bright new heights

When my world was overshadowed by clouds
you painted over the grey with vibrant colour

When I am alone and scared at what lies ahead
you remind me that you will always remain at my side
even when I turn down the next dark lane

Kelly Van Nelson

ARRIVAL HALL

Frosted glass blocking view
Jaws of double doors slide open and closed
People coming out
Nobody going in

One-way traffic moves at snail pace
Bodies fatigued from cramped conditions
Faces glowing from sunshine
Eyes flat, knowing they might not pass through
The jaws again for some time

Another coffee to pass the time
Toss disposable cup in the trash
Fidget in chair screwed to the floor
This place is maddening

You walk through
Pushing suitcase on metal trolley
I run to you and fall into your arms –
Kiss you
Taste coffee on your lips, or is it on mine?
So glad you have arrived
All is familiar again

AWAY SONG BIRD

Push and pull
Push me away
Away from home
Away I ran
Ran amok
Ran aground
Aground and safe
Aground and lost
Lost at sea
Lost and found
Found salvation
Found a friend
Friend in need
Friendly face
Face is kind
Face is mean
Mean and lean
Mean machine
Machine learning
Machine gun
Gunpowder
Gunshot
Shot up
Shot down
Down in the dumps
Down and out
Outcast
Outlast
Last leg
Last man standing
Standing firm
Standing tall
Tall boy
Tall order

Order of events
Order around
Around the block
Around the law
Law and order
Law of the land
Land of the living
Land of the free
Free from you
Free as a bird
Bird song
Bird soars
Song
Soars

RED OR DEAD

Hope is a Banksy red balloon
Floating away from oppression
I am a red balloon
Floating away from you

Kelly Van Nelson

AN ODE TO A BULLY

Your words are cruel
thick with spite
dark molasses
sticking to the skull

Your nudges are cruel
hard and unkind
peanut brittle
caught between teeth

Your rumours are dangerous
nasty fodder
toffee morsels
tasty and chewy

Your intent was misplaced
to bring down the weak
sweet sustenance
made me stronger

HOUSEBOUND

Been housebound for some time
These windows form a prism
The bricks, the mortar, walls and doors
Detain me like a prison

Daily soup, it has no taste
The liquid, sustenance
I sip, I mess, I must confess
In simple things repentance

This chair, viewpoint for life
Until the day I die
Young and alert, frail and old
In dignity I'll lie

A car crash snatched my freedom
My will, my legs, my heart
It rubber-stamped my future
Left me with no standing start

The cruel hand of fate
Grabs me in my sleep
Sweat, shiver, shake and wake
Beg happiness to make a peep

My father and mother breathe no more
They made it to the grave
Deserted me, their only child
Heaven denied, cruel twist of fate

Here I am and here I'll stay
Until my time has come
No point wallowing in self-pity
When all is said and done

Kelly Van Nelson

Wheeled on stage, a mic in front
Hold crowd in paralysed hand
Recall the night I steered the wheel
Into tree in no-man's land

Tanked that night, I hid it well
Picked parents up on way
They climbed in back, we laughed and joked
Drink-driving doesn't pay

Standing ovation, I finish my speech
Memories blurred, but message clear
Audience rises while I never will
To the law, hope they adhere

ANIMAL KING 'DOM'

Primate male monkey business
dominant baboon
slapping and biting
Christian Grey of the jungle
ensuring subservience
thrusting perceived strength
to show who is on top

Domestic bird
flaunting cock
hen's cage fighting
who will rule the rooster?
alpha chicken pecks orders to flock
beta chicken endows Alpha a wide berth
unafraid to rustle every other feather

Lustrous machoness meerkat
territorial hunter
moving in on her man
digging in claws
watching for predators
immune to venom
stamping out intense breeding competition

Juvenile male elephants
elderly gents in musth breed
excessive testosterone
unable to overthrow matriarchal system
females banish errant masculine bully
forcing spurt from erect trunk
playing girl-on-girl instead

Kelly Van Nelson

Omega wolf
bottom of the pack
scapegoat for whipping
shackled servant of vented frustration
howling with injustice
gaining satisfaction in providing social glue
preserving structure through every
perfectly formed full moon

WAR 'VERSES' PEACE

War imposed on others through armed conflict
Battles between governments, gangs, communities, states, countries
Uniformed soldiers obey command to impose death sentence
Mercenaries and militia dicing with life
Violence and destruction irrecoverable
Suffering and mortality in combat and fatal friendly mistake

V

Peace stimulating harmonious well-being
Individual and heterogeneous civilians
Free from disturbance
Living as one in tranquillity
Without hostile aggression and any fear of
Suffering and mortality from combat and fatal friendly mistake

STEP BACK TO EXISTENCE

books stolen
called names
tripped up
put down
lied about
punched hard

      felt weak
      felt outcast
      felt sad
      felt afraid
      felt pain
      felt non-existent

            told a teacher
            told a friend
            told a stranger
            told my sister
            told my mum
            told my dad

                  books found
                  apology accepted
                  stood up for myself
                  brushed myself down
                  truth told
                  punched goals

REJOICE

revenge is never sweet
the taste that's left is bitter
sinking to low levels
only adds to the litter

the laughs are all on me
give respect where it is due
you showed none in the past but
now I'm living life without you

SILVER LINING

The silver helium balloon has been shrivelling over the last few days. It was hand-delivered, tied to a beautiful bouquet of bright yellow sunflowers – the only flowers I've received lately that weren't woven into a wreath. So thoughtful of my sister to send them a few weeks after Mark's funeral. She's an angel. Added in a note that the sun will eventually shine in my life once again. The kindness from everyone else has faded. No more casseroles left on my front step. People have their own problems to deal with. Not that I'm seeking ongoing sympathy, but becoming a widow in my twenties was so unexpected. Pull my blonde hair into a ponytail. Feels greasy. Can't remember when I last washed it. Tug on a tracksuit and my runners; force myself to venture out to pick up a few essential groceries. When I get to the mall, I'm drawn to a gift shop selling candles and condolences cards. End up buying another silver helium balloon. When I get home, I'm unable to stop crying as I stare at it. After a while, I get up and fetch a carving knife from the wooden block in the kitchen. Think about slicing into my wrists. Checking out would be the easiest way to run away from my problems. Instead, I poke a tiny hole in the neck of the balloon and put my mouth over it. I suck the air out, hoping to become light enough to float up to Heaven to see Mark. Instead, I become lightheaded. A laugh escapes my lips, high-pitched and uncontrollable. It snowballs into a bout of hysteria ricocheting around the walls of my apartment. So glad the helium balloon has a silver lining.

Published by Lapidus International, a not-for-profit organisation promoting wellness and good mental health

OPPORTUNITY KNOCKS

taking every new opportunity
opportunity when it does come knocking
knocking it clean out of the park
park the past, now is time, it's not shocking

moving forward to where pastures are greener
greener grass, growing strong, fills the field
field of dreams, life is there for the taking
taking every new opportunity

WORKING-CLASS LASS

Council terrace overdue for renovation
Roughcast housing for a rough cast

Broken bottles decorate concrete jungle
Green glass substitute for green grass

Commotion outside – juvenile joyriders burning rubber
Cop 'copter circling above waiting to cop a kill

Geordie jails occupied by too many old school friends
Big Market breeding small-time criminals

Keep myself busy picking wood chips out of bedroom wallpaper
No place for chips – not even on the shoulder

Gypsy tarot reading in the back of funfair wagon at The Hoppings
Grass greener than green glass on other side of moor fence

Spark catches in Saltwell Park on Guy Fawkes Night
Fire in belly watching kaleidescope of fireworks cartwheel

One-way ticket out of the 'Toon'
No more *Magpies* matches after I fly the nest

Never crossed the Tyne Bridge to return to Newcastle-Upon-Tyne
But at heart I'll always be a working-class lass

SET ADRIFT

sails down, a lost vessel adrift at sea
motion sickness from the sway of emotions
water leaks in cracks – no longer able to plug
the drowning of the soul

bail out, diving into icy cold waves
swim against the current
fight against the desire to sink
gasp for air as dry land nears

wash up, exhausted, on the beach
catch breath, basking in the sun
dry out, skin tingling with anticipation
of what might be inland

stretch and stand on my feet
dust off gritty sand
stroll towards the unknown
thirsty, yearning for hydration

gulp in life and all it offers
alone, learn to love myself
no longer care he doesn't love me back
body revitalised, mind free, soul fulfilled

INIMITABLE

In the morning you rise with a smile on your face

Never wasting a moment on negative energy

In the evenings you look back on the difference you've made that day

Mindful always of others

In the darkest hours of the night you dream of boundless peace

Tossing and turning in angst that you have not done enough

Always concerned for others, never yourself

Best-in-class at leading by example

Loving and caring for those in your life

Endless is my respect for the inimitable gem that you are in this world

COMPASS NORTH

Fork in life as you stab with sharpened knife
Not fazed at rubbish spurting from your mouth
Salt of the earth as you pepper with hate
My compass points due north as you tug south

Open book while you close doors with cruel words
Big ideas trailblazing your small mind
My spade's a spade; go shovel your own sh*t
Why thrive on being bitter and unkind?

Sunrise mitigates your mood in sunset
Circle of friends outside circle of fire
Attract white knight as you wallow in black
Love struck while pain inflictions transpire

Beauty inside out; ignore ugly intent
Inner peace as you tool up for world war
Enjoy simple life, avoiding your maze
Break through ceiling as you stamp foot on floor

Float to shore as heavy weight makes you sink
Free as a bird as you flap in your cage
Directing my own script while you act up
Backstage – your narcissism centre stage

Live electricity – your spark is dead
My compass north. Can't you point there instead?

Kelly Van Nelson

NO PLACE LIKE HOME

Putting down fresh roots
growing in unfamiliar
soil in wild garden
surrounding this strange new house –
my home is where the heart is

Graffiti Lane

THE GAMBLE

See a penny, pick it up
All day long you'll have good luck
Roll the dice and land on six
Take a gamble, pick-up-stix
Twenty-one, stick or twist
Chances taken, others missed

Penny foolish, pound wise
See the truth amidst the lies
Walk away when it's your time
Do not waste another dime
Life's too short to take too long
In gambling on something wrong

RINGMASTER

between iron bars
glimpses of life
meander along concrete corridor
engrossed in staying alive or
waiting to die: who knows?

across plastic table
screwed to the floor
momentous glances connect
the weakest lowers eyes
the strongest licks upper lip in anticipation

no clowning around today
instead pinned down by acrobatic gang helping
ringmaster tame the lion
roll up, roll up!
be entertained by the roaring beast
being whipped and defiled

hidden in the big tent
enduring inhumane bullying as cowards
brutally abuse imbecile white-collar
inmate who avoided the tax man
forever paying the price with freedom

penetrating the heart, stabbing with shard
until blood oozes from my perpetrator who is
fighting tooth and nail
while justice prevails
an eye for an eye

SPRING CLEAN

Let go of the past.
Time to clear junk from cupboards –
making space for spring

AFFIRMATION

I am defeated
Before the whistle blows
In this battle of the wills

Stand toe to toe
I don't look up
For fear of the eye of the tiger

Mind is blank
Body is numb
As I go through the motions

A week passes
Each morning staring in the mirror
Telling myself I am good enough

Affirmation to combat
Psychological warfare
With no other enemy but myself

Inner calm takes hold
Energy is centred
Nerves will not get the better of me

I am a winner
When the whistle blows
In this battle of the wills

WILLPOWER

Kneel in prayer, asking for one blessing:
Lord, please grant me willpower this day
to never lose the big dreams
residing in my soul
to complacency.
Let me be
forever
trying
hard.

RISE

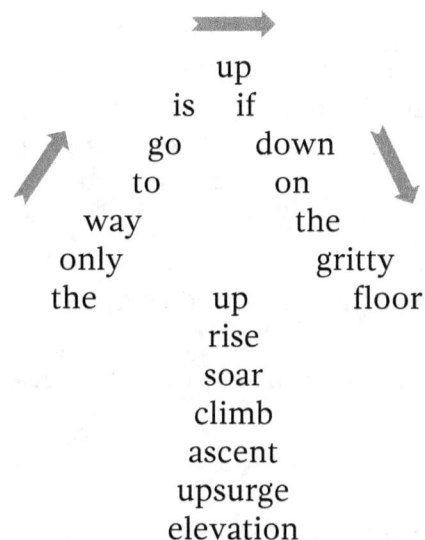

```
                →
             up
          is  if
         go   down
         to   on
        way   the
       only   gritty
        the   up    floor
              rise
              soar
              climb
              ascent
              upsurge
              elevation
```

Graffiti Lane

SUBVERSIVE EPIGRAMS

Inscriptions of ancient past
Figure drawings on sepulchres
In underground catacombs of Rome

Unearthed in excavations of Pompeii
Scratched public notices and spontaneous messages
Legible ramblings preserved

In the Greek city of Ephesus
Classical images advertising the wares of
A ripe woman for sale

Carved symbols in the tombs of Egypt
Declarations of undying love
Capturing simple thoughts of an otherwise forgotten life

Satirist Arab poems
Written political rhetoric
Manifesting hatred towards unwanted regimes

Illicit contemporary messages in urban New York
Blatantly positioned in public view
Across subways and bridges

Iconographic murals on Belfast, Berlin, West Bank walls
Voicing opinions in times of conflict
Uniting or dividing communities

Subversive epigrams spread like rats from England
Government TAG on anti-social behaviour
Banksy #anon talks back

Controversy across the globe
Social and political ideals conveyed
Vandalism or art?

Kelly Van Nelson

Today's inscriptions become tomorrow's ancient past
Scribbles waiting to be found in the dust
Rising from underground catacombs

PHANTASMAGORIA

I am dazzled by
the kaleidoscope of love
you spray upon me

THE IMMIGRANT

Winded, from life's punches
Family feuds, financial pressures, final straws
Unable to load any more on these

                                              weary shoulders

Sails fill with nature's energy
Steering the vessel towards new beginnings
Hope for a better life blows gently over

                                                tingling skin

Red, white and blue Australian flag
Flapping in the breeze atop the tallest of poles
Sense of belonging forms with matronly country
Accepting of a stranger in her

                                                soft bosom

Flying colourful kite
Catching gusts of wind on a cloudy day
Turn smiling face to emerging sun; carefree foreigner with

                                                wild hair

Kelly Van Nelson

ME, MYSELF AND I

I am me
Happy in this skin
Content with myself
At peace in my own company
Relishing what gifts each day brings
Embracing the unknown future with open arms
Excited to share my thoughts with the world
Proud I have something important to say
Accepting of my past
For it shaped me
Into who I am
I am me

SMILE

Smile wide
Be different
with pride

Smile more
It's infectious
you know

Smile bright
In this crazy world
delight

NELSON'S COLUMN

Rising high in commemoration
granite column astoundingly tall
constructed to command passer-by attention
it silently touches them all

Reminding the world of Third Coalition War
tasteful rather than vulgar.
Immense statue, honouring death –
blood spilled in Battle of Trafalgar

Built to last centuries, historical architecture
pedestal to hat, tall and bare
stony ghost stands, facing due south
over London's infamous square

An admiral then and admirable now
his deeds in history matter.
Immense statue, honouring death –
blood spilled in Battle of Trafalgar

Horatio Nelson died in 1805
motionless, tranquil, at rest.
Life carries on, bustling by
pigeons making their nest

Wings still as they rest on his shoulder
birds sharing their chatter.
Immense statue, honouring death –
blood spilled in Battle of Trafalgar

A naval engagement, twenty-seven
formidable ships in British fleet.
Lord Nelson aboard HMS Victory
courageously led on his feet

Kelly Van Nelson

Refusing to be bullied by
French and Spanish navies in anger.
Immense statue, honouring death –
blood spilled in Battle of Trafalgar

GROWTH SPURT

lost
girl grows
confidence
becoming woman
found

PIGTAILS

hair braided in two tight plaits
not one loose thread
permitted to be
unruly and free

little girls should be seen not heard
not a single word
escapes young lips
life an eclipse

grow up determined to succeed
typing at speed
cut off pigtails
sharing my tales

MUSICAL YOUTH

no silver spoon in this boy's mouth
just a radio humming in the background
my folks were the backing singers in my life
neither taking the lead

joined the school band
played classic guitar solo
until the popular kids
made me go solo in the playground

tossed in the towel on the private lessons
caused a rift with the tutor
too many riffs to master
prefer to scale up creativity time instead

calloused fingers defiant
colourful plucks strewn on every surface
discarded so the steel strings can
form grooves on my skin

clamp the capo on a precise fret
shortening the strings
lifting the sound to a higher pitch
to distract me from the mental fret

over and over I strum the chords
until a chord strikes in my head
this is my only outlet
music is my saviour

find a new tutor a suburb away
move to the electric
plug in the amp
far enough away nobody hears the notes

Kelly Van Nelson

master Metallica
no sheet music
just me in the moment
nothing else matters

talent competition in senior year
sick of getting grief for hair being too long
jot my name on the registration
legit reason for letting my hair down

stage bright with spotlights
take a spot in the middle
unleash the pent-up anger
rewarded with a standing ovation

onslaught of hassle to join the school band
since blowing them away with the electric solo
don't cave to peer pressure from the popular kids
me and my guitar are going someplace else

one-way ticket to the big smoke
busk the streets by day
sleep the streets by night
not having to commute is the ultimate work perk

move from outside to inside
smoky clubs and backstreet bars
upload a tune online
thumbs up

made the big time
everyone remembers my name
see my folks in the front row and smile
took me a long time to remember who bought me my first guitar

ONE OF A KIND

You can't intimidate me

                                        Can't imitate me

I am me

Black
Mask over face
Not to protect my identity
But to prevent toxic fumes filling my lungs
I shake the can and let loose across brick as day breaks

STREET ART

                      The commissioned work takes me until nightfall
                          A breath of fresh air is filling my lungs
                                As I spray my identity
                                    Mask over wall
                                        White

Graffiti Lane

WEEDS

woke this morning
pulled on the suit
glanced out the window

at the immaculate lawn
with perfectly manicured borders
and pretty flowers in full bloom

in the office the plants are plastic
easy maintenance, low cost
investments that never wilt, in line with frugality strategy

head to a conference
speak on stage
share advice on how to GROW our business

realise how far I've travelled
to leave behind the concrete slab
of my childhood

recall how we all
struggled at school:
truanting, taunting, taunted

back at my beechwood desk I
ask Google to find contact details
of my old headmaster

want to offer to conduct a
motivational speech
in my old home town

to high school girls
underprivileged, undernourished
some likely under the influence

Kelly Van Nelson

find images of dilapidated school
shut down last year
due to insufficient grades

weeds sprawling the grounds
where I once tried to
dodge hockey sticks from bruising my ankles

have so much to say
to these forgotten girls
set adrift without an olive branch

this is my new stage
these pages covered with
rambling ivy

where weeds flourish the soil is fertile
perfect for cultivating seeds of hope
that will bloom in the wilderness

Success Elements

Drink *water* from the fountain of knowledge
Let the *wind* fill your sails every day
Let the *fire* in the belly take hold
Stay down to *earth*, plant feet, don't lose your way

TURNING THE TABLES

Why did you once make a girl cry?
Your words slashed deep
Now watch her soar and fly

She always turned away in silent goodbye
Didn't trust herself to speak
Why did you once make a girl cry?

Walking school corridors with eyes never dry
Unable to maintain composure
Now watch her soar and fly

You awarded yourself the right to probe and pry
Her life became public property
Why did you once make a girl cry?

Heavy head once low is now held high
Every taunt injected strength
Now watch her soar and fly

Are the tables turned as you read words so wry?
Does it hurt to have your flaws exposed?
Why did you once make a girl cry?
Now watch her soar and fly

VA-VA-VOOM

Electricity generates when you walk in the room
Explosive, you lift others with a loud boom
Sweeping away negativity with your broom
Never spiralling with doom and gloom
A racing car with incredible va-va-voom
A pocket rocket on the way to the moon
Reputation preceding you, making others swoon
A miracle from the day you grew in the womb
Forever the prettiest rose in full bloom

Kelly Van Nelson

DREAMS
desires
ambitions

the past is long gone
a colourful future
somewhere over the rainbow

"your pot of gold is awaiting"

TECHNOPHOBIA

Two tennis balls, elastics, skipping rope
Running wild outdoors with a dirty face and no curfew
Unwrap Christmas present – Commodore 64
Addictive games on cassette
Playtime moves from outside to inside head
Imagination boundless
Freestyle era

Mum buys a computer with a dot matrix printer
Monitor almost as large as the fridge
Reams of paper with perforations down both edges
She teaches me how to type – wondrous machine
Self-teach myself to communicate via binary code
0110100101101
Clever era

Leave school, get a job using a fax machine
Paper everywhere; kill a tree each day – Messages in/Messages out
Noisy machine – bleeping instils recipients with a sense of importance
Succinct messages about coffee orders and stationery supplies
Regret not applying for employment in the
Espionage industry cracking state secrets
Eager era

The 'internet' is here
Surf the World Wide Web
Email the receptionist every morning to say hello
Create a filing system for messages sent back
Do / Delegate / Delete
Efficient era

Kelly Van Nelson

Promoted into Y2K Meltdown Prevention Team
Triple figure emails daily – Ping!
Impossible to maintain
Do / Delegate / Delete
Miss the old fax machine
Company buys new mainframe and bigger servers
Test daily for Y2K bugs, document risks
12:01am 1st January 2000 comes and goes
Green light stays on
No code reds
Bored era

Upskill in web development
Establish own business, invaluable experience on my CV
Designed several websites for .com industry
Boom!
New sports car with sat nav
House with high-spec burglar alarm and remote-controlled gate
Slimline phone with built-in mega-pixels camera
Capture life in the fast lane
Successful era

Sold business and paid off mortgage
Joined corporate giant in senior 'leadership' role managing:

Vision
　Purpose
　　Values
　　　Strategy
　　　　Sales
　　　　　Delivery
　　　　　　People
　　　　　　　Budgets
　　　　　　　　Customers
　　　　　　　　　Investors
　　　　　　　　　　Stakeholders
　　　　　　　　　　　Shareholders
　　　　　　　　　　　　Redundancies
　　　　　　　　　　　　　Market analysis
　　　　　　　　　　　　　　Technology enablement
　　　　　　　　　　　　　　　Employee disengagement

MS Outlook out of control rendering me with no other outlook
Overwhelmed era

Boss gives me upgraded smartphone for Christmas bonus
Real-time emails 24/7
Do / Delegate / Delete
Anytime, anyplace, anywhere
Set up rules, automatically send messages to digital filing cabinet
Implement new leadership strategy – monthly 'email-free day'
Educate colleagues to stroll over to people's desks for conversation
Encourage face-to-face interaction
Collaborate and build interpersonal relationships
Hit every target
Replace old sports car with new wheels
Fulfilled era

Promoted, given new slimline laptop
Installed with video conferencing facilities
Upset there can be no more conference calls in my pyjamas
Travel frequently, store important files on USB kept in laptop case
Leave laptop bag in airport lounge
Human Resources investigation regarding:

Privacy Act
   Data breach
      Data privacy
         Data protection
            Consumer Rights
               Information Security
                  Corporate Espionage

Always knew I was destined to be a spy
Served notice
No more Do / Delegate / Delete
System login disabled
CTRL / ALT / DEL
Dumb era

Find inner Zen
Trade in coffee for green tea
Pick up pen and notebook – A paper notebook!
~~Scribble nonsense and score it out~~
Scribble brilliant insights – in ink!
Handwrite a poem
Experiment with stanza layout
Abort rhyming patterns
Imagination boundless when working with no boundaries
Freestyle era

AMBITION OF AN AUTHOR

dream in the day not just at night
think like there is no box
rise knowing there is no ceiling
write because your heart knows it's right

ROADBLOCKS

Leaves flutter to ground,
settling in autumn mounds.
I skip straight through them.

LOVE BETWEEN THE LINES

A prosaic first poem inside a card
Roses are red

A limerick verse with humorous connotation
Are violets blue or violet?

Rhythmic flow with a smoothness of beat
Sugar is sweet

Evocative meaning, aesthetically pleasing
So are you xxx

WINNING GAME

Pawn in battle, could improve
Bishop diagonal, fit in groove
Rook don't mess around, straight-laced
Knight in shining armour, raced
Queen of destiny, nothing to prove
King to checkmate, strategic move

Kelly Van Nelson

ON THE CHIN

You used to feel hurt at the names you were called
You used to find bystander silence left you appalled
You used to get told you were too fat or too thin
You used to turn a blind eye and took abuse on the chin

You once were a child who sat on her own
You once found words hurt you more than a stone
You once suffered depression at what had transpired
You once gave up hope when overwhelmingly tired

You soon found a way to stand on your two feet
You soon took a place at a table with a seat
You soon met new people who saw you in a different light
You soon learned to live without feeling the fight

You never told a soul about the hard times you faced
You never wanted sympathy, instead the future embraced
You never gave up on those hopes that you dreamed
You never lost faith no matter how hard it seemed

Graffiti Lane

DIAMOND IN THE ROUGH

an outer skin of tenderness
        not immune to shallow cuts or a cowardly bruise
                inflicted by a small-minded bully
                      healing quickly by finding muse
                              perpetually resilient
                                      until death

                                in life
                    forever sparkling
              even when the going gets tough
        capable of cutting through the hardest obstacles
    diamond in the rough, radiant and rare
an inner strength; proudly unbreakable

Kelly Van Nelson

SOLITARY SUPERSTITION

I don't believe horseshoes bring good fortune
Or lucky rabbit's foot
The power of four leaf clovers
Or knocking hard on wood

I don't avoid number thirteen
Or black cat crossing path
Or dread broken mirror brings bad luck
Seven years relentless wrath

I don't think rainbows bring pots of gold
Or absence makes the heart grow fonder
Am happy to walk under the ladder
Spilt salt never thrown over shoulder

We bring on our own good luck
Through passion and hard work
I do however say 'God Bless'
My faithful little quirk

Graffiti Lane

DAYS OF SUMMER

Dreams fill winter's nights –
Hard work fills days of summer
in fierce pursuit.

ONLY YOU

Only you can let somebody
put you down and make you cry

Only you can spread your wings
so you can finally soar and fly

Only you can let your past
define your life today

Only you can hold you back
from what you're meant to say

SPACE ODYSSEY: BEYOND TOMORROW

Space:
    Limitless thoughts jostling inside head until
    steam bursts from ears to create black hole
    substantial enough for cogs to turn
    stimulating a supernova from the myriad of
    floundering ideas to spark genius scream
    Eureka!
    Psychedelic brainwave leaving audience electrocuted in a
    galaxy
    gasping for air

Infinity:
    Ocean's tide churning murky mystery as
    waves surge in and out gathering
    immeasurable particles of sand
    crushed into oblivion with nature's mortar and pestle
    over millions of years rendered into something capable of
    slithering between impotent fingers
    impossible to grasp

Strength:
    Mighty force incubating inside shell
    poised to erupt when kicked in a spurt of
    resilience surfacing in the face of adversity
    majority operating on positive nib of durable batteries
    minority combusting in brutish anger
    bullies abusing power in the palm of cowardly hands

Kelly Van Nelson

Willpower:
>   Determination to bask in bright sunshine
>   shoot for the stars and land on the moon
>   conquering four corners of the universe where possibilities
>   cascade over the edges in a constant waterfall
>   tumbling into a wishing well brimming with dreams
>   never ceasing to make them a reality until the soul is
>   drowning in fulfilment

Love:
>   Selfless consideration of another human being
>   richer than a precious gem held in highest esteem
>   above and beyond
>   imaginable realms of reality perched on
>   golden pedestal of respect and trust
>   entrenched within beating heart until
>   death do us part

Odyssey:
>   Innocent baby forever
>   seeded in my mind's eye
>   familiar masterpiece created to spawn
>   immortal journey of another alien generation
>   in the beginning, foetus infiltrating womb
>   in the middle, assaulting senses
>   in the end life, prevailing for eternity

ENCORE!

It's time to flourish and thrive
    Live life to the fullest of ability
Not allowing the past to deprive
    A future awaits, filled with tranquillity

Live life to the fullest of ability
    Enjoy spontaneity in the here and now
A future awaits, filled with tranquillity
    Encore! Take your well-earned bow

Enjoy spontaneity in the here and now
    Take centre stage, rightful place for a star
Encore! Take your well-earned bow
    Rightfully yours, always destined to go far

Take centre stage, rightful place for a star
    It's time to flourish and thrive
Rightfully yours, always destined to go far
    Not allowing the past to deprive

Kelly Van Nelson

GRAFFITI LANE

Author
sprays lane
with graffiti

Editor
attempts intervention

It's a dead end

ACKNOWLEDGEMENTS

The long and winding laneways tackled by a writer can be a daunting maze, with many twists and turns leading to dead ends. It has been liberating to finally turn a corner and find a light shining brightly on *Graffiti Lane*.

First and foremost, thank you, Karen Mc Dermott for shining that light. You have the kindest heart and are my guardian angel. Your early belief in my writing began with the publication of one of my short stories via Serenity Press and provided the solid foundations upon which my career is now being built. I know we will keep adding creative bricks, climbing ladders, and shouting words that matter aloud from the rooftops. That one email you sent me that simply said, 'WOW', after reading my manuscript submission gave me the magical boost I needed. I would dearly love to spray-paint that WOW on every wall in the land!

Clive Newman, my hero at The Newman Agency, I am eternally grateful that you took the time to peek inside my pages and for your unwavering belief in my abilities as an author. Your advice is always perfectly timed and sound in logic. I will keep writing, editing and polishing to hone my craft to be the best it can possibly be.

Teena Raffa-Mulligan, your attention to detail and meticulous editing process is nothing short of amazing. Every suggestion you made was gold dust, sprinkling my manuscript with the professional touch it needed. What a pleasure being able to leverage your expertise.

Designing the cover for this book was a mini-project managed by the incredibly talented Thomas Paul Woodward, who also created my website. Tom, you deserve a medal for your patience trawling through hundreds of images of graffiti-adorned buildings from the photo shoot and applying so many variations of contemporary graphical effects. The end result perfectly captures the essence of my gritty author brand in an edgy, eye-catching cover – Love your work @thomaspaulartistry.

Paul Unstead, thanks for inspiring Hosier Lane to be the cover location with your incredible PunkB&W photography.

To the beautiful Tess Woods – where do I start? It was destiny joining your Wales Winter Writing Retreat on a last-minute whim. You have taught me so much. How to brutally kill my darlings, market my work, and come up with way better book titles. Thanks for steering me towards this one – it rocks! You told me you would pull up a front row stool and watch the show. I will keep refining my skills until the production is a sell-out. It was also no coincidence that you handed me Karen Mc Dermott's book, *Mindful Magic*, in Wales, which I devoured in front of a roaring fire as snowflakes fell outside the window. I'm indebted to you for the intro to Karen that got me onto the first rung of the Australian publishing ladder. A special thanks to your family too, for their hospitality and warmth. To the amazing authors on the retreat, Anna, Enisa, Joanne, Joanie, and Kerry, your constant encouragement means the world to me.

My growth as a writer has also been greatly assisted by all at the Katharine Susannah Pritchard Writers' Centre - what a difference you have made to my life. To have been awarded the KSP First Edition Fellowship as part of an emerging writers program, funded by the Western Australian Department of Local Government, Sports and Cultural Industries and Lotterywest, is a gift for which I am eternally grateful. Thank you to Fremantle Press for the insightful workshops and events offered as part of the program. Lisa Wolstenholme – thank you for making it so easy to settle into KSP in the early days and for your ongoing support since.

I'm also privileged to belong to the KSP Writefree Women's Writing Group. I joined this eclectic and talented bunch of fellow writers in early 2018 and never looked back. Each one of you superhuman ladies gave me the boost of confidence to try new submission avenues, resulting in publication success in the USA, UK and Australia. Hoping for that red-carpet moment with you all so we can sip a glass of bubbly in style. A special thanks to Barbara Gurney, who peer-reviewed an early draft of several of the poems contained in this collection and gave me priceless guidance.

There are so many fellow authors who offered ongoing support along the road to publication. I am indebted to you for pointing me in the right direction. The Australian writing community surely is one of the finest incubators on earth for selfless coaches and mentors. Rachael Johns, Natasha Lester, Michael Trant, Holden Sheppard, Louise Allan, Michelle Johnston, Michelle Dennis, Scott-Patrick Mitchell - You let me into your inner circle with the warmest of welcomes and have kept me focused and motivated ever since. Dr Laurie Steed, thanks for your kind note when it was most needed, nudging me to take the next step – this is that step.

Jacqui Campbell-Howard, Verity Wilson and Jacki Rafter, you have been musketeers at my side from the beginning, lifting the spirits (literally) when it seemed my efforts were fruitless. Your friendship and smiling faces in the crowd at book launches are truly a blessing.

To the numerous other early supporters and readers of my work, thank you for believing in my writing, often more than I believed in it myself. Special acknowledgement goes to Bill and Mas O'Neil, Grace and Colin Hilditch, Laura and Stuart Nisbet, Luke 'sponsor' Johnson, Angela Evans, Emma Bailey, and the Liwara and SHC parents who I leaned on for moral support along the way. Also appreciate everything top-notch book bloggers and local author champions do. Massive thanks to Michelle Greening, Tracey Gregory, Jacie Anderson, Maureen Eppen and Amanda Barrett.

Craig Gaffney, thanks for introducing me to art produced by HUSH. To the street artists who reached out about my poetry collection, or who I took creative liberties to TAG after seeing your talented designs on my travels, you are awesome. Banksy, you have inspired me to add a trip to Palestine to my bucket list.

To the politicians who have approved street art projects, thank you for your brave stance in supporting a contemporary art form often misunderstood. Differentiating between legal and illegal forms of graffiti is never easy. These initiatives go a long way in helping educate the public on how the graffiti sub-culture can have a positive impact upon the community through youth engagement and the development of talented young artists' skills.

Rafael Moyano, Givile Mockute and the executive team, Anna Moolman, Dr Margot Wood, Karyl Treble, Kevin Alexander, and all of my other peers at The Adecco Group, I owe you endless gratitude for propping me up and allowing me creative space. Ian Grundy, thanks for the mentoring and brand guidance. Cameron Knox, you were a couple of years too soon introducing me to your book club (lol), but the debut is finally here. Omar Alim, the whisky poem made it!

Ger Doyle and Erica Page, you sent me up the Swiss Alps carrying the heaviest of baggage and provided the footholds to climb down again carrying the lightest feather quill. I found myself and my writing mojo up that mountain!

To my sister Joanne and the Henderson's, Roy, Sandra, the Van Nelson and Doubell gangs, thanks for the family support and laughs along the way. I can never take myself too seriously with you lot around.

Shaun, my soulmate, for years it has been you, me and the laptop. You patiently (and occasionally impatiently) put up with my fingers constantly tapping at computer keys, my nose always buried in a book, my bouts of insomnia where I scribble until dawn, and the crazy thought process I bring into our family that sometimes overshadows normal life. Without you, my world would be black and white.

Imani and Kayin, thank you for listening to my poems when nobody else would, giving me the inspiration to chase my dreams, always believing I would get this book onto the shelves, and for being the best kids in the universe. I love you to space odyssey and beyond.

ABOUT THE AUTHOR

Kelly Van Nelson is a fiction author from the North East of England who lived in Edinburgh, London, and Cape Town before immigrating to Australia. She has had multiple poetry and short stories featured in publications in the UK, USA and Australia (Serenity Press, Short Story Society, United Press, Between These Shores Books, Fiction War Magazine, Wolvesburrow Productions, KSP Writefree Women's Writing Group). She is represented by Clive Newman at The Newman Agency.

Graffiti Lane is her powerful debut poetry collection. As well as success as a poet, Kelly has also received multiple accolades for her manuscript, *The Pinstripe Prisoner*, which placed third in the Yeovil Literary Prize, shortlisted in the Wales PENfro first chapter competition, and longlisted in the Exeter Novel Prize. In December 2018 she was awarded a First Edition Fellowship through Katharine Susannah Pritchard Writers' Centre. The fellowship is part of an emerging writer pilot program funded by the Western Australian Department of Local Government, Sports and Cultural Industries and Lotterywest.

Kelly is also the mum of two children, wife of her soulmate of more than two decades and the managing director on the executive board of a multi-national organisation. In short, she is a juggler.

Website: www.kellyvannelson.com
Facebook: https://www.facebook.com/kellyvannelsonauthor
Twitter: https://twitter.com/kellyvannelson
Instagram: https://www.instagram.com/kellyvannelson
LinkedIn: https://www.linkedin.com/in/kellyvn